EMMANUEL JOSEPH

The Fractured Mirror, Piecing Together Confidence, Identity, and Inner Peace

*Copyright © 2025 by Emmanuel Joseph*

*All rights reserved. No part of this publication may be reproduced, stored or transmitted in any form or by any means, electronic, mechanical, photocopying, recording, scanning, or otherwise without written permission from the publisher. It is illegal to copy this book, post it to a website, or distribute it by any other means without permission.*

*First edition*

*This book was professionally typeset on Reedsy.*
*Find out more at reedsy.com*

# Contents

| | | |
|---|---|---|
| 1 | Chapter 1: A Shattered Reflection | 1 |
| 2 | Chapter 2: The Roots of Insecurity | 2 |
| 3 | Chapter 3: The Journey of Self-Acceptance | 3 |
| 4 | Chapter 4: Embracing Vulnerability | 5 |
| 5 | Chapter 5: The Power of Authenticity | 6 |
| 6 | Chapter 6: Reclaiming Your Voice | 7 |
| 7 | Chapter 7: The Role of Self-Discovery | 9 |
| 8 | Chapter 8: Navigating the Waters of Change | 10 |
| 9 | Chapter 9: Building Resilience | 12 |
| 10 | Chapter 10: The Art of Letting Go | 14 |
| 11 | Chapter 11: Cultivating Self-Love | 15 |
| 12 | Chapter 12: The Journey of Healing | 16 |
| 13 | Chapter 13: Embracing Gratitude | 17 |
| 14 | Chapter 14: The Power of Purpose | 18 |
| 15 | Chapter 15: The Importance of Mindfulness | 19 |
| 16 | Chapter 16: The Journey of Self-Expression | 21 |
| 17 | Chapter 17: The Ongoing Journey | 22 |

# 1

# Chapter 1: A Shattered Reflection

In the beginning, life feels like a mirror—reflecting back at us who we are and what we believe. Yet, often, that reflection becomes fractured. When we look into the mirror, we see not a cohesive image but pieces of ourselves scattered. This fragmentation is the starting point of our journey, the point where confidence, identity, and inner peace seem distant, elusive dreams.

It is in the moments when life throws its harshest storms at us that our reflection shatters the most. We question our worth, our abilities, and our very essence. The voices of doubt grow louder, and we feel as though we are losing ourselves in the cacophony. However, it is through this breaking that we can begin to piece together a stronger, more resilient version of ourselves.

As we start to gather the pieces of the fractured mirror, we realize that each shard holds a story, a lesson, and an opportunity for growth. Our task is to find the courage to confront these pieces and embrace them as parts of our journey. It is in this process of acceptance and understanding that we start to rebuild our confidence and reclaim our identity.

In the silence that follows the storm, we find clarity. We begin to see that the fractured mirror is not a symbol of brokenness but of transformation. It is an invitation to embark on a journey of self-discovery, where each piece we gather and mend brings us closer to inner peace. Through this journey, we learn to see the beauty in our scars and the strength in our imperfections.

# 2

# Chapter 2: The Roots of Insecurity

Our journey towards confidence, identity, and inner peace often begins with exploring the roots of our insecurities. These roots are often deeply embedded in our past experiences, shaping our beliefs and perceptions of ourselves. It is essential to unearth these roots to understand how they influence our present and to begin healing.

Insecurity often stems from moments of rejection, failure, and criticism. These experiences plant seeds of doubt that grow into towering fears. We internalize these negative experiences, allowing them to define our self-worth. Over time, these insecurities become the lenses through which we view ourselves and the world, distorting our perception and limiting our potential.

By delving into our past, we can identify the moments that have shaped our insecurities. This process requires vulnerability and honesty, as we confront painful memories and acknowledge the impact they have had on us. It is through this introspection that we can begin to untangle the web of insecurities and challenge the negative beliefs that have taken root within us.

As we uncover the roots of our insecurities, we also discover the power to transform them. By reframing our experiences and recognizing our resilience, we can begin to rewrite our narrative. We learn that our worth is not defined by our past but by our ability to grow and evolve. In doing so, we lay the foundation for building confidence, reclaiming our identity, and finding inner peace.

# 3

# Chapter 3: The Journey of Self-Acceptance

Self-acceptance is a pivotal step in our journey towards confidence, identity, and inner peace. It involves embracing all aspects of ourselves, including our flaws, vulnerabilities, and strengths. This process requires compassion and patience, as we learn to love ourselves unconditionally.

The path to self-acceptance is often fraught with obstacles. We are conditioned to strive for perfection, to hide our imperfections, and to seek validation from external sources. This relentless pursuit of an unattainable ideal leaves us feeling inadequate and disconnected from our true selves. To break free from this cycle, we must shift our focus inward and cultivate self-compassion.

Self-compassion involves treating ourselves with the same kindness and understanding that we would offer to a loved one. It means acknowledging our struggles, forgiving ourselves for our mistakes, and celebrating our achievements. By practicing self-compassion, we create a nurturing environment in which we can grow and thrive.

As we embrace self-acceptance, we begin to see ourselves in a new light. We recognize that our worth is not contingent on our achievements or the approval of others but is inherent in our being. This realization empowers us to live authentically, to honor our values and desires, and to pursue our dreams with confidence. Through self-acceptance, we find the peace and fulfillment we have been seeking.

# 4

# Chapter 4: Embracing Vulnerability

Vulnerability is often perceived as a weakness, something to be avoided or hidden. However, it is through embracing our vulnerability that we can truly connect with ourselves and others. By allowing ourselves to be seen and heard, we open the door to deeper understanding, empathy, and growth.

Vulnerability involves exposing our true selves, including our fears, doubts, and insecurities. It requires courage to lower our defenses and let others see our imperfections. In doing so, we create space for authentic connections, where we can be accepted and loved for who we are, rather than who we think we should be.

Embracing vulnerability also means being honest with ourselves. It involves acknowledging our emotions, rather than suppressing or denying them. By facing our fears and insecurities head-on, we can begin to understand their origins and work through them. This process allows us to build resilience and develop a deeper sense of self-awareness.

As we embrace vulnerability, we begin to see it as a source of strength rather than a weakness. We realize that our willingness to be open and authentic is a testament to our courage and resilience. Through vulnerability, we cultivate empathy and compassion, both for ourselves and others. In doing so, we create a foundation for genuine connections and a deeper sense of inner peace.

# 5

# Chapter 5: The Power of Authenticity

Authenticity is the cornerstone of confidence, identity, and inner peace. It involves living in alignment with our true selves, honoring our values, and expressing our unique gifts. By embracing authenticity, we can navigate life with a sense of purpose and fulfillment.

Living authentically requires us to let go of societal expectations and the need for external validation. It means embracing our individuality and trusting our intuition. This process involves shedding the masks we wear to fit in and embracing our true selves, flaws and all. In doing so, we create a life that is genuine and meaningful.

Authenticity also involves being true to our values and principles. It means making choices that align with our beliefs, even when it is challenging or unpopular. By staying true to ourselves, we build integrity and self-respect. This, in turn, boosts our confidence and reinforces our sense of identity.

As we live authentically, we inspire others to do the same. Our courage to be ourselves creates a ripple effect, encouraging those around us to embrace their true selves as well. Through authenticity, we create a supportive and empowering environment, where everyone can thrive. In doing so, we contribute to a world where inner peace and fulfillment are attainable for all.

# 6

# Chapter 6: Reclaiming Your Voice

In the cacophony of external influences and expectations, our inner voice often gets drowned out. Reclaiming our voice is a crucial part of our journey towards confidence, identity, and inner peace. It involves tuning into our inner wisdom and expressing our truth with authenticity and courage.

Our inner voice is our compass, guiding us towards our true north. It whispers our dreams, desires, and values, urging us to live in alignment with our authentic selves. However, over time, this voice can become muffled by the noise of societal expectations, fear of judgment, and self-doubt. Reclaiming our voice requires us to quiet the external noise and reconnect with our inner wisdom.

One of the most powerful ways to reclaim our voice is through self-expression. Whether it is through writing, speaking, art, or any other medium, expressing our thoughts and feelings allows us to honor our truth. It is an act of courage that reinforces our identity and builds confidence. By sharing our stories and perspectives, we also create opportunities for connection and understanding.

As we reclaim our voice, we become more attuned to our intuition. We learn to trust ourselves and our decisions, knowing that our inner wisdom is a reliable guide. This process empowers us to navigate life with confidence and clarity, staying true to our values and aspirations. Through reclaiming our voice, we strengthen our sense of self and cultivate inner peace.

# 7

# Chapter 7: The Role of Self-Discovery

Self-discovery is a lifelong journey that involves exploring and understanding our true selves. It is through self-discovery that we gain insights into our strengths, weaknesses, passions, and values. This process is essential for building confidence, defining our identity, and finding inner peace.

The journey of self-discovery often begins with introspection. By reflecting on our experiences, thoughts, and emotions, we can gain a deeper understanding of who we are. This process requires honesty and self-awareness, as we confront both the light and shadow aspects of ourselves. Through introspection, we can identify the patterns and beliefs that shape our behavior and choices.

Self-discovery also involves exploring new experiences and stepping out of our comfort zones. By trying new activities, meeting new people, and challenging ourselves, we expand our horizons and uncover hidden talents and passions. This process allows us to redefine our limitations and embrace our potential, building confidence in the process.

As we embark on the journey of self-discovery, we learn to appreciate our unique qualities and celebrate our individuality. We recognize that our worth is not defined by comparison to others but by our authenticity and growth. This realization brings a sense of inner peace, as we embrace our true selves and live in alignment with our values and desires.

# 8

# Chapter 8: Navigating the Waters of Change

Change is an inevitable part of life, and learning to navigate it with grace is essential for building confidence, identity, and inner peace. Change can be both exhilarating and daunting, as it often requires us to let go of the familiar and embrace the unknown. By developing resilience and adaptability, we can navigate the waters of change with confidence and clarity.

Change often brings uncertainty and challenges, which can trigger fear and resistance. However, it is through facing these challenges that we grow and evolve. By viewing change as an opportunity for growth rather than a threat, we can shift our perspective and approach it with a positive mindset. This shift in perspective allows us to embrace change with openness and curiosity.

One of the keys to navigating change is to stay grounded in our values and beliefs. By staying true to ourselves and our principles, we can make decisions that align with our authentic selves, even in the face of uncertainty. This sense of alignment provides a stable foundation from which we can navigate change with confidence.

As we navigate the waters of change, it is also important to practice self-care and compassion. Change can be stressful and overwhelming, and it is essential to prioritize our well-being. By taking care of ourselves and seeking support when needed, we can build resilience and maintain our inner peace. Through resilience and adaptability, we can navigate change with grace and emerge stronger and more confident.

# 9

# Chapter 9: Building Resilience

Resilience is the ability to bounce back from adversity and adapt to challenges. It is a key component of confidence, identity, and inner peace. Building resilience involves developing a mindset and skillset that allows us to navigate life's ups and downs with strength and grace.

One of the foundations of resilience is a positive mindset. This involves cultivating optimism and focusing on solutions rather than problems. By viewing challenges as opportunities for growth, we can approach them with a sense of curiosity and determination. This positive mindset allows us to navigate adversity with resilience and confidence.

Another important aspect of resilience is developing coping skills. This involves learning healthy ways to manage stress and emotions, such as mindfulness, exercise, and seeking support. By developing effective coping strategies, we can maintain our well-being and navigate challenges with greater ease.

Building resilience also involves nurturing our relationships and support networks. By surrounding ourselves with supportive and understanding individuals, we create a strong foundation from which we can draw strength. These connections provide emotional support and a sense of belonging, which are essential for building resilience and maintaining inner peace.

As we build resilience, we learn to trust ourselves and our ability to navigate adversity. We recognize that challenges are a natural part of life and that we have the strength and resources to overcome them. This sense of confidence and self-trust allows us to face challenges with courage and grace, fostering a sense of inner peace and fulfillment.

# 10

# Chapter 10: The Art of Letting Go

Letting go is an essential part of the journey towards confidence, identity, and inner peace. It involves releasing the things that no longer serve us, such as past traumas, negative beliefs, and unhealthy relationships. By letting go, we create space for new growth and opportunities.

The art of letting go begins with acknowledging what we are holding onto and understanding how it impacts our lives. This process requires self-awareness and introspection, as we identify the patterns and behaviors that keep us stuck. By recognizing these influences, we can begin to disentangle ourselves from them and move forward.

Letting go also involves forgiveness, both of ourselves and others. Holding onto grudges and resentments only weighs us down and prevents us from finding peace. By practicing forgiveness, we free ourselves from the burden of negativity and create a sense of inner harmony. This act of compassion allows us to heal and move forward with a lighter heart.

As we let go of what no longer serves us, we make room for new possibilities. We open ourselves to new experiences, relationships, and opportunities for growth. This process empowers us to live in the present moment, fully embracing our potential and creating a life that aligns with our true selves. Through the art of letting go, we find freedom and inner peace.

# 11

## Chapter 11: Cultivating Self-Love

Self-love is the foundation of confidence, identity, and inner peace. It involves nurturing and caring for ourselves, both physically and emotionally. By cultivating self-love, we build a strong sense of self-worth and create a fulfilling and meaningful life.

Cultivating self-love begins with self-care. This involves prioritizing our well-being and making time for activities that nourish our body, mind, and soul. Whether it is through exercise, meditation, hobbies, or spending time with loved ones, self-care allows us to recharge and maintain our energy and vitality. By taking care of ourselves, we show that we value and honor our needs.

Self-love also involves setting healthy boundaries. This means recognizing our limits and protecting our time and energy. By setting boundaries, we create a safe and supportive environment in which we can thrive. This act of self-respect reinforces our sense of self-worth and empowers us to live authentically.

As we cultivate self-love, we also practice self-compassion. This involves treating ourselves with kindness and understanding, especially during challenging times. By offering ourselves the same compassion we would extend to a friend, we create a nurturing and supportive inner dialogue. This practice strengthens our resilience and fosters a sense of inner peace.

# 12

# Chapter 12: The Journey of Healing

Healing is an integral part of the journey towards confidence, identity, and inner peace. It involves addressing and processing past wounds, whether they are physical, emotional, or psychological. By embarking on the journey of healing, we can release the pain and trauma that hold us back and create a path towards wholeness and fulfillment.

The journey of healing often begins with acknowledging and accepting our pain. This process requires courage and vulnerability, as we confront the difficult emotions and memories that we may have suppressed. By allowing ourselves to feel and express our pain, we create space for healing and transformation.

Healing also involves seeking support and resources. Whether it is through therapy, support groups, or self-help books, accessing the right tools and guidance can facilitate our healing process. By reaching out for support, we show that we are committed to our well-being and growth.

As we heal, we also develop new coping strategies and resilience. This involves learning healthy ways to manage stress and emotions, such as mindfulness, journaling, or creative expression. By developing these skills, we can navigate life's challenges with greater ease and maintain our inner peace. Through the journey of healing, we reclaim our power and create a sense of wholeness and fulfillment.

# 13

# Chapter 13: Embracing Gratitude

Gratitude is a powerful practice that can transform our perspective and enhance our sense of confidence, identity, and inner peace. By focusing on the positive aspects of our lives and expressing appreciation, we can cultivate a mindset of abundance and fulfillment.

Embracing gratitude begins with shifting our focus from what is lacking to what is present. This involves recognizing and appreciating the blessings, big and small, that enrich our lives. By acknowledging the positive aspects of our experiences, we create a sense of contentment and joy.

Practicing gratitude also involves expressing our appreciation to others. Whether it is through a simple thank you or a heartfelt note, expressing our gratitude strengthens our connections and fosters a sense of community. This practice not only enhances our relationships but also reinforces our sense of self-worth and belonging.

As we embrace gratitude, we also develop resilience. By focusing on the positive aspects of our lives, we build a foundation of strength and optimism that helps us navigate challenges. This positive mindset allows us to approach life with confidence and inner peace, knowing that we have the resources and support we need to thrive.

# 14

# Chapter 14: The Power of Purpose

Finding and living with purpose is a transformative experience that can enhance our confidence, identity, and inner peace. Purpose gives our lives meaning and direction, guiding our actions and decisions. By aligning with our purpose, we create a sense of fulfillment and joy.

The journey to discovering our purpose often begins with introspection and self-reflection. It involves exploring our passions, values, and talents, and considering how we can use them to make a positive impact. This process requires us to be honest with ourselves and to listen to our inner wisdom.

Living with purpose also involves setting goals and taking intentional actions. By setting clear and meaningful goals, we create a roadmap for our journey. These goals provide motivation and focus, helping us to stay aligned with our purpose. By taking intentional actions, we move closer to our aspirations and create a life that reflects our true selves.

As we live with purpose, we also inspire and uplift others. Our passion and commitment create a ripple effect, encouraging those around us to pursue their own dreams and aspirations. Through the power of purpose, we contribute to a more connected and empowered world, where inner peace and fulfillment are within reach for all.

# 15

# Chapter 15: The Importance of Mindfulness

Mindfulness is a powerful practice that can enhance our confidence, identity, and inner peace. It involves being fully present in the moment, with a non-judgmental awareness of our thoughts, feelings, and experiences. By cultivating mindfulness, we can navigate life with greater clarity, resilience, and joy.

Mindfulness begins with the practice of paying attention to the present moment. This involves observing our thoughts and emotions without getting caught up in them. By bringing our awareness to the here and now, we create a sense of calm and clarity. This practice allows us to respond to life's challenges with greater ease and composure.

Mindfulness also involves cultivating a sense of curiosity and acceptance. This means embracing our experiences, both positive and negative, with an open and non-judgmental attitude. By accepting our experiences as they are, we reduce stress and create a sense of inner peace. This practice allows us to navigate life with greater resilience and adaptability.

As we cultivate mindfulness, we also develop a deeper connection with ourselves and others. By being fully present in our interactions, we create more meaningful and authentic connections. This practice fosters empathy and compassion, both for ourselves and others. Through mindfulness, we enhance our sense of confidence, identity, and inner peace.

# 16

# Chapter 16: The Journey of Self-Expression

Self-expression is a vital aspect of our journey towards confidence, identity, and inner peace. It involves sharing our thoughts, feelings, and creativity with the world. By expressing ourselves authentically, we reinforce our sense of self and create a fulfilling and meaningful life.

The journey of self-expression begins with exploring our passions and interests. This involves identifying the activities and pursuits that bring us joy and fulfillment. Whether it is through writing, art, music, or any other form of creative expression, these activities allow us to connect with our true selves and share our unique gifts with the world.

Self-expression also involves embracing our individuality. This means honoring our unique perspectives, experiences, and talents. By expressing ourselves authentically, we create a sense of integrity and self-respect. This practice boosts our confidence and reinforces our sense of identity.

As we embrace self-expression, we also create opportunities for connection and understanding. By sharing our stories and perspectives, we invite others to see and appreciate our true selves. This practice fosters empathy and compassion, both for ourselves and others. Through self-expression, we enhance our sense of confidence, identity, and inner peace.

# 17

## Chapter 17: The Ongoing Journey

The journey towards confidence, identity, and inner peace is a lifelong process. It involves continuous growth, self-discovery, and transformation. By embracing this journey, we create a fulfilling and meaningful life that reflects our true selves.

The ongoing journey requires us to remain open to new experiences and challenges. This means embracing change and uncertainty with curiosity and resilience. By viewing life as a continuous process of growth, we create a sense of excitement and possibility. This perspective allows us to navigate life's ups and downs with greater ease and grace.

The journey also involves nurturing our relationships and connections. By surrounding ourselves with supportive and understanding individuals, we create a strong foundation from which we can thrive. These connections provide emotional support and a sense of belonging, which are essential for building confidence and inner peace.

As we continue on our journey, we also practice self-compassion and self-care. This means prioritizing our well-being and treating ourselves with kindness and understanding. By nurturing ourselves, we create a sense of inner harmony and fulfillment. Through the ongoing journey, we cultivate a life that is rich in confidence, identity, and inner peace.

**Description:** Embark on a transformative journey with "**The Fractured Mirror: Piecing Together Confidence, Identity, and Inner Peace.**" This insightful book delves into the challenges of self-discovery and personal growth, offering readers a roadmap to navigate life's complexities with resilience and grace.

Through seventeen thoughtfully crafted chapters, the book explores the roots of insecurity, the power of vulnerability, and the importance of self-acceptance. It highlights the significance of authenticity, self-expression, and purpose in building a fulfilling and meaningful life. With each chapter, readers are guided to embrace their unique qualities, set healthy boundaries, and cultivate self-love.

"The Fractured Mirror" also emphasizes the role of gratitude, mindfulness, and resilience in achieving inner peace. It provides practical strategies for coping with change, healing past wounds, and reclaiming one's voice. By integrating these principles into daily life, readers can develop a strong sense of confidence and identity.

This book is a beacon of hope and inspiration for anyone seeking to create a life that reflects their true selves. It invites readers to embark on a journey of self-discovery, where they can find strength in their imperfections and beauty in their scars. Through the pages of "The Fractured Mirror," discover the path to inner peace and fulfillment.

www.ingramcontent.com/pod-product-compliance
Lightning Source LLC
LaVergne TN
LVHW020508080526
838202LV00057B/6240